FRENCH FASHION PLATES
in Full Color from the
GAZETTE DU BON TON
(1912–1925)

58 Illustrations of Styles by
Paul Poiret, Worth, Paquin and Others

As Rendered by
GEORGES LEPAPE, GEORGE BARBIER
et al.

DOVER PUBLICATIONS, INC.
NEW YORK

ACKNOWLEDGMENT

The publisher wishes to express his thanks to

MR. BENJAMIN BLOM,

who conceived of this volume and made its realization
possible through the loan of his complete run of the
Gazette du Bon Ton.

FRONT COVER: ON THE CLIFF (*Sur la falaise*): summer dress by
Redfern; drawn by J. (Francisco Javier) Gosé [Aug. 1913, Plate
VII]. Red and gray Athenian silk tulle; coral clasp at the waist.

*French Fashion Plates in Full Color from the Gazette du Bon Ton
(1912–1925)* is a new work, first published by Dover Publications, Inc.,
in 1979.

International Standard Book Number: 0-486-23805-9
Library of Congress Catalog Card Number: 79-50347

Manufactured in the United States of America
Dover Publications, Inc.
180 Varick Street
New York, N.Y. 10014

PUBLISHER'S NOTE

One of the handsomest and most influential of all fashion magazines was the Parisian *Gazette du Bon Ton,* which appeared with several interruptions between November 1912 and December 1925. It was founded by the active French journalist Lucien Vogel, whose whole life was devoted to high-class periodical publications, with an emphasis on fashion. His father, Hermann Vogel, was a noted draftsman whose imaginative work appeared for years in the prestigious satirical magazine *L'Assiette au Beurre.* Before launching the *Gazette du Bon Ton* at the age of 26, Lucien Vogel had already been artistic director of *La Vie heureuse* and editor-in-chief of *Art et Décoration.* After the *Gazette* he went on to other journals, particularly the *Jardin des Modes,* which he continued to publish even after the Second World War.

The text of the *Gazette* consisted of urbane articles, copiously illustrated with vignettes, on theater, travel and other topics of interest to the leisured wealthy, but with clothing and personal adornment always as the paramount subject. The real heart of each monthly issue, however, was the plates. Drawn by a brilliant pleiad of artists, many of them youthful (the illustrators A.-E. Marty and Pierre Brissaud got their start on the *Gazette*), these lavish plates depicted the latest confections of the ultra-chic *maisons de haute couture* of the period: Paquin, Paul Poiret, Worth, Lanvin and a highly select group of others. The magazine both created and recorded fashion history in the crucial years from the sumptuous twilight of the *belle époque* through the typical look of the mid-Twenties: sheath dresses and boyish bobs.

The 58 illustrations in the present volume comprise a choice cross section of plates from the entire run of the magazine, representing the chief artists and couturiers.

Emphasis has been placed on actual women's wear: afternoon and walking dresses for different seasons and locales, evening gowns, tailored suits, coats and cloaks, muffs and hats, and even pajamas. In addition, there are a few dresses for young girls, one theatrical costume and a handful of the inventive party costumes that were such a characteristic phenomenon of the days preceding the First World War. The caption to each plate contains the following elements wherever applicable: the original French title of the plate, with English translation; the type of garment and the couturier; the artist responsible for the plate; the issue of the *Gazette* in which the plate originally appeared, with the original plate number;* and a slightly abridged translation (omitting no information) of the original French description of the plate, including the cut of the garment, materials, colors and details of trim.

It is hoped that costume designers, historians of clothing and general culture, and admirers of commercial art at its absolute acme, will all find this selection an inexhaustible resource for research and pleasure.

* The "first year" of the *Gazette* ran from November 1912 to October 1913, and the plates of each monthly issue were numbered afresh from I to X. The "second year" ran from January 1914 through June ("Summer") 1915; from that "year" on, the plates ran consecutively throughout the "year" as Arabic numbers—except for the ten plates of January 1914, which had Roman numbers. The war interrupted publication, and the "third year" coincided with the calendar year 1920 (in 1920, month indications were dropped—there were only ten yearly issues from then on—and our captions indicate only issue numbers). The "fourth year" was 1921, the "fifth" was 1922. After another gap (during which the directorship passed from Vogel to Jean Labusquière), the "sixth year" ran from June 1923 to June 1924, and the "seventh" and final "year" (with only nine issues) ran from July 1924 to December 1925.

INDEX OF ARTISTS

INDEX OF COUTURIERS, MILLINERS AND BOOTMAKERS

AT THE COMEDY (*A la Comédie*): theater wrap by Paquin; drawn by J. (Francisco Javier) Gosé [Nov. 1912, Plate VII]. Old-pink watered silk (moire) and black velvet adorned with Japanese embroideries; the skunk collar reaches to the waist.

LASSITUDE: dinner gown by Paul Poiret; drawn by Georges Lepape [Nov. 1912, Plate VIII]. White soft velvet covered with a tunic of black tulle embroidered with polychrome flowers.

HAVE I COME TOO EARLY? (*Serais-je en avance?*): theater wrap by Paul Poiret; drawn by Georges Lepape [Dec. 1912, Plate VI]. Cobalt-yellow silk trimmed with skunk; the arm slits and the clasp are embroidered in the same shade and allow the blue-green satin lining to be seen.

THE EMPTY CAGE (*La Cage vide*): dinner gown by Redfern; drawn by A(ndré)-E.
Marty [Dec. 1912, Plate VII]. Draped tunic of Japanese crepe with brocaded chry-
santhemums, over a sheath of *lumière*-green charmeuse.

THE ANTIQUE MIRROR (*Le Miroir ancien*): evening gown by Paquin; drawn by Maggie [Jan. 1913, Plate V]. Fire-red silk muslin, and a drapery of bengaline [corded fabric of silk possibly mixed with cotton or wool] with gold embroidery and filigree.

TOO MUCH TO CHOOSE FROM (*L'Embarras du choix*): tailored suit by Paul Poiret; drawn by Georges Lepape [Jan. 1913, Plate VI]. Muted green cloth with Veronese green edgings; braiding of black velvet, bright steel buttons; the jacket is puckered at the waist by a rolled hem of velvet forming a sort of half-belt; otter collar.

WOMAN AND PUPPETS (*La Femme et les pantins*): marionettes; drawn by
Georges Lepape [Feb. 1913, Plate II]. Pleated gold-gauze skirt beneath a brass-frame
skirt of Persian brocade. The pantalets and the long-sleeved blouse are of pleated silk
muslin with gold bracelets at the wrists, ankles and neck.

FROM THE APPLE TO THE LIPS (*De la Pomme aux lèvres*): masquerade costume by Redfern; drawn by Charles Martin [Feb. 1913, Plate VI]. The princess gown of close-woven velvet, studded with silver spangles, opens in the front to reveal a silk muslin underdress.

A CHINESE WOMAN (*Une Chinoise*): party costume by Doeuillet; drawn by
Pierre Brissaud [Feb. 1913, Plate IX]. Red and black cloak, lined with silk, covering
a satin pannier over a silk skirt with embroidered garland; underdress of crepe de
chine.

THE LADIES' ADVISER (*Le Conseiller des dames*): theater gown and wrap; drawn by George Barbier [March 1913, Plate I.] Gown of marquisette [sheer fabric of light silk or lustrous cotton] worked with silver; silk wrap with large brocade motifs.

AFTER THE SHOWER (*Apres l'ondée*): dinner gown by Worth; drawn by A. Lorenzi [Apr. 1913, Plate V]. Aeolian silk trimmed with tulle over a double skirt of soft velvet.

THE CHERRIES (*Les Cerises*): country outfit by Paul Poiret; drawn by Georges Lepape [May 1913, Plate IX]. Embroidered white crepon [firmer than crepe, silk possibly mixed with wool or cotton] trimmed with tussah silk; Italian straw hat trimmed with silk ribbon and small embroidered flowers.

THE ANTIQUE MINIATURE (*La Miniature ancienne*): dinner gown by Redfern; drawn by Bernard Boutet de Monvel [May 1913, Plate X]. Dress of charmeuse; tunic of blonde lace, trimmed with a Circe bayadere belt, over a pleated tulle bodice.

THEY'RE LOOKING AT US (*On nous regarde!*): new summer muffs; drawn by
Georges Lepape [July 1913, Plate I]. Walking muffs, one of silk flowers, the other
of wool embroidery.

BY MOONLIGHT (*Au Clair de la lune*): evening wrap by Paul Poiret; drawn by
Georges Lepape [July 1913, Plate VII]. Silk wrap adorned with colored embroidery
and lined with satin.

GOODNESS, HOW COLD IT IS (*Dieu! qu'il fait froid . . .*): winter coat by Paul Poiret; drawn by Georges Lepape [Oct. 1913, Plate IV]. Cut silk velvet trimmed with skunk.

LE JARDIN DU PEYROU: tailored suit by Chéruit; drawn by Bernard Boutet de Monvel [Jan. 1914, Plate VI]. Jacket of rough or nubby wool in a two-tone plaid; serge skirt; civet-cat trim on collar and sleeves; small belt at waist, half serge and half leather.

THE AUTUMN CROCUSES (*Les Colchiques*): traveling cloak by Paquin; drawn by George Barbier [Jan. 1914, Plate IX]. Rough or nubby wool, with a velvet vest and a fur collar.

ALMS (*L'Aumône*): fancy tailored outfit; drawn by Georges Lepape [Feb. 1914, Plate 11]. Taffeta skirt and cloth-of-gold bolero.

"COROMANDEL": evening wrap and gown; drawn by George Barbier [Feb. 1914, Plate 12]. Wrap of velvet with fur trim; gown of chiffon trimmed with rhinestones, finished at the bottom with rhinestone fringes and embellished with a short chiffon tunic over a white crepe-de-chine slip.

POSING FOR A PORTRAIT (*La Séance de portrait*): tailored outfit by Worth;
drawn by Bernard Boutet de Monvel [Feb. 1914, Plate 14]. Brown velvet lined with
brick-red crepe de chine and trimmed with fox.

THE FOSTER SISTERS (*Les Soeurs de lait*): afternoon dress by Doeuillet; drawn
by A(ndré)-E. Marty [Feb. 1914, Plate 17]. Navy-blue serge with pleated tunic;
little blouse of white satin and candy-striped belt.

WOMAN PLAYING A THEORBO (*La Joueuse de Théorbe*): evening wrap by
Paquin; drawn by George Barbier [Feb. 1914, Plate 18]. Black velvet and pink velvet,
trimmed with silver lace and edged with gray fox at the sleeves and bottom of skirt.

THE SEASHELL FOUNTAIN (*La Fontaine de coquillages*): evening gown by
Paquin; drawn by George Barbier [March 1914, Plate 27]. Gray tulle with gray
beads over a turquoise velvet sheath.

"SALOMÉ": evening gown by Paul Poiret; drawn by Sim(one)-A. Puget [March 1914, Plate 28]. Pleated black tulle on a white ground, embroidered with little jet studs; the body suit of black lace; the top of white tulle edged with jet.

THE STUNNING LITTLE FISH (*L'étourdissant petit Poisson . . .*): summer dress; drawn by George Barbier [May 1914, Plate 44]. White silk dress with pink stripes, underneath a double gauze skirt; straw hat trimmed with coral balls.

LOVE CAGED (*L'Amour en cage*): afternoon dress; drawn by J. Van Brock [June 1914, Plate 54]. Walking dress with flounces of checked taffeta; cashmere shawl trimmed with fox.

| A | B | | C | D | | E |

FIRST VICHY GROUP, OR ALL OF YOU BEHAVE! (*Vichy* [1] *ou Soyez tous bien sages*) [the plates in this issue illustrated clothing that was actually exhibited—in three sections: "Vichy," "Longchamp" and "Côte d'Azur"—at the San Francisco Panama-Pacific International Exposition of 1915]; drawn by George Barbier [Summer 1915, Plate 2]. A: Small girl's dress by Paquin; white tulle; blue taffeta jacket. B: Woman's outfit by Doucet; yellow cambric with ruffles from shoulders to hips; the side panels of the coat, embellished with white lace, reveal the tightly pleated skirt; hat by Georgette. C: Woman's outfit by Beer; very wide dress of white lawn with large *fond-de-bonnet* Beauvais lace trimmings; navy-blue bolero of thick silk with blue velvet revers; hat by Lewis; shoes by Greco. D: Girl's outfit by Chéruit; ivory satin coat with pronounced puckers at the sides; belt of the same material;

F   G   H   I   J

squirrel collar. E: Woman's outfit by Martial et Armand; very wide sky-blue taffeta
with "hoop" pleats at the sides only; the bodice has a round cut-out neckline beneath
a Frans Hals collar of lawn with openwork trimming; hat by Camille Roger; shoes
by Ducerf. F: Girl's outfit by Chéruit; "alb" of embroidered and pleated tulle and
muslin over an underdress of faded-blue taffeta. G: Girl's outfit by Chéruit; chemise
of flesh-colored marceline [thin silk fabric] trimmed with silver. H: Woman's outfit
by Premet; hand-embroidered white muslin dress; two-tiered skirt striped with white
braid; three-shade candy-striped belt; hat by Maria Guy. I: Woman's outfit by Callot;
white linen dress over a blue satin slip; the flounces are of appliqué work on tulle,
the bodice of plain tulle. J: Girl's outfit by Callot; chemise dress of pink tussah silk
with white embroidery; hat by Callot.

AVENUE DU BOIS: drawn by Drian [Summer 1915; unnumbered, undescribed plate].

MLLE. PAULETTE DUVAL: theatrical costume by Doeuillet; drawn by Barjansky [Feb. 1920, Plate 5]. Costume of Spanish dancer for the production *L'Heure exquise* at the Théâtre Michel; orange taffeta and sapphire-blue velvet embroidered with gold and jade.

TANGIERS, OR THE CHARMS OF EXILE (*Tanger ou Les Charmes de l'exil*): afternoon dress and cape by Paul Poiret; drawn by Georges Lepape [Feb. 1920, Plate 7]. Both garments are of heavy Moroccan sackcloth; white-embroidered seams and wool pompoms; the belt is a Gallo-Roman copper armband; the straw sunbonnet is the typical headgear of the women of Tangiers.

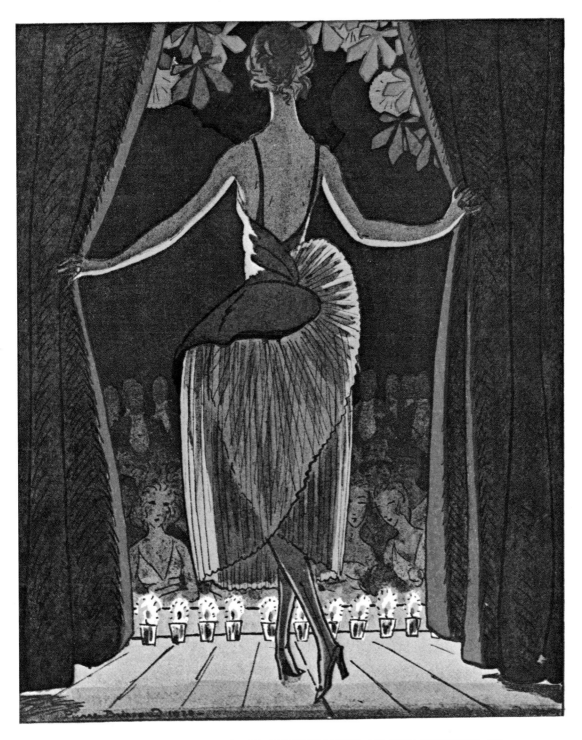

THE PROLOGUE, OR AMATEUR PERFORMANCE AT THE COUNTRY ES-
TATE (*Le Prologue ou La Comédie au château*): drawn by Pierre Brissaud [July
1920, Plate 40]. Evening gown of midnight-blue charmeuse with a skirt of pleated
pink tulle.

WALKING ON MONTMARTRE (*La Promenade à Montmartre*): ensemble by
Beer; drawn by Charles Martin [1920, issue 9, Plate 68]. Dress of "bishop-violet"
charmeuse with red edgings; black velvet cape with violet lining and otter collar.

PARISIAN ENCUMBRANCES (*Les Embarras de Paris*): afternoon coat by Doeuillet; drawn by A(ndré)-E. Marty [1920, issue 9, Plate 69]. Two-piece tailored coat of navy-blue cheviot wool with red embroidery and red cloth collar.

SMOKE (*Fumée*): evening gown by Beer; drawn by George Barbier [1921, issue 1, Plate 8]. Black satin embroidered in white, gray and silver.

THE MILKY WAY (*La Voie lactée*): evening gown and cape by Worth; drawn by George Barbier [1921, issue 3, Plate 22]. Cape of pomegranate marocain [ribbed fabric of silk or wool], the fringes caught up with rhinestone motifs, the collar of curled speckled feathers; the dress is a wraparound of gold sultania ending in a long train, over a black crepe-de-chine skirt; long fringes and rhinestone epaulets.

FAREWELL! (*Adieu!*): evening wrap by Worth; drawn by George Barbier [1921, issue 4, Plate 28]. Black velvet with wide steel-spangled bands and narrower black-spangled bands; puckered velvet collar tied with two ribbons held by rosettes of waxed satin and florets.

AT (*A*) PALM BEACH: tailored outfit by Worth; drawn by George Barbier [1921, issue 5, Plate 40]. Three-piece outfit of red poplin; bodice of muslin covered with blue lace; jacket of poplin embroidered with navy blue.

DINNER AT THE COUNTRY ESTATE (*Le Dîner au château*): evening wrap by
Paul Poiret; drawn by A(ndré)-E. Marty [1921, issue 6, Plate 46]. Black satin;
collar embroidered with stones.

LA BELLE DAME SANS MERCI: evening gown by Worth; drawn by George Barbier [1921, issue 6, Plate 47]. Marocain adorned with blue velvet flowers over a tunic of silk fringe.

CON MOLTO SENTIMENTO: evening gown by Paul Poiret; drawn by A(ndré)-E. Marty [1921, issue 8, Plate 60]. Green satin embellished in front with a quasi-apron of ostrich plumes of the same shade.

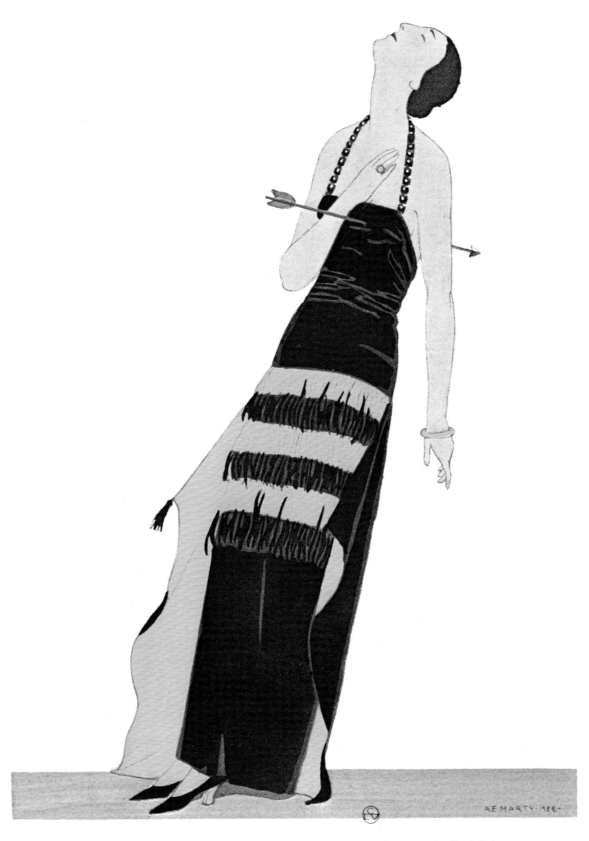

RIGHT THROUGH THE HEART (*En plein Coeur*): evening gown by Paul Poiret;
drawn by A(ndré)-E. Marty [1922, issue 2, Plate 12]. Black velvet trimmed with
jet; panels lined with green crepe de chine.

THE INOPPORTUNE SHOWER (*L'Averse intempestive*): Riviera dress by Worth;
drawn by George Barbier [1922, issue 2, Plate 14]. Black marocain lined with marocain of cock-of-the-rock orange.

WHO COULD HELP LOVING YOU? (*Qui ne vous aimerait?*): evening gown by
Worth; drawn by George Barbier [1922, issue 4, Plate 28]. Lamé, with tassels of
black silk worked with rhinestones and red beads.

IT IS I (*C'est moi*): evening wrap by Paul Poiret; drawn by A(ndré)-E. Marty [1922, issue 5, Plate 39, undescribed].

THE MIRROR, OR A PASSING GLANCE (*La Glace ou Un Coup d'oeil en passant*): evening wrap by Paul Poiret; drawn by A(ndré)-E. Marty [1922, issue 6, Plate 47, undescribed].

VESPER: evening gowns by Worth; drawn by George Barbier [1922, issue 8, Plate 60]. Left: beaded black georgette [thin silk crepe with pebbly texture] over a gold lamé sheath. Right: draped gown of gold lamé, with belt of stones and pink taffeta ribbon.

WITCHCRAFT (*Sortilèges*): evening gown by Beer; drawn by George Barbier [1922, issue 9, Plate 66]. Skirt of tinted beads beneath silver lace; top of muslin embroidered with rhinestones over a silver slip.

ROSALINDE: evening gown by Worth; drawn by George Barbier [1922, issue 10, Plate 75]. Gold lace with a beaded belt adorned with fringes of beads.

STUDIES IN RED (*Sanguines*): evening gowns by Worth; drawn by George Barbier
[1923, issue 4, Plate 16, undescribed].

WHAT! READY SO SOON? (*Comment? . . . déjà prête!*): evening gown and pajamas by Jeanne Lanvin; drawn by Georges Lepape [1924, issue 7, Plate 39, undescribed].

THE INFANTA'S ROSE (*La Rose de l'Infante*): costume by Worth; drawn by George Barbier [1924, issue 8, Plate 42, undescribed].

IN THE CONSERVATORY (*Dans la Serre*): dancing dress by Madeleine Vionnet; drawn by Thayaht [1924, issue 10, Plate 55, undescribed].

PEEKABOO! (*Coucou!*): dress by Paul Poiret; drawn by A(ndré)-E. Marty [1924/
5, issue 1, Plate 1, undescribed].

HERE I AM! (*Me voici!*): dress by Worth; drawn by George Barbier (1924/5, issue 1, Plate 3, undescribed].

THE ADVISER (*Le Donneur de conseils*): evening gown by Paul Poiret; drawn by
A(ndré)-E. Marty [1924/5, issue 5, Plate 34, undescribed].

VENUS AND THE GRACES WITH BOBBED HAIR (*Les Grâces et Vénus en cheveux courts*): evening wrap and gowns by Paul Poiret; drawn by A(ndré)-E. Maity [1924/5, issue 2, Plate 9, undescribed].